W9-BMG-289

DISCARD

SONIA

SOTOMAYOR

Essential Lives

Sonia Sotomayor

Supreme Court Justice

by Martin Gitlin

Content Consultant
Alixandra B. Yanus, PhD
High Point University

ABDO
Publishing Company

CREDITS

Published by ABDO Publishing Company, 8000 West 78th Street, Edina, Minnesota 55439. Copyright © 2011 by Abdo Consulting Group, Inc. International copyrights reserved in all countries. No part of this book may be reproduced in any form without written permission from the publisher. The Essential Library™ is a trademark and logo of ABDO Publishing Company.

Printed in the United States of America,
North Mankato, Minnesota
052010
092010

Editor: Rebecca Rowell
Copy Editor: Paula Lewis
Interior Design and Production: Kazuko Collins
Cover Design: Kazuko Collins

Library of Congress Cataloging-in-Publication Data
Gitlin, Marty.
  Sonia Sotomayor : Supreme Court justice / Martin Gitlin.
      p. cm. — (Essential lives)
  Includes bibliographical references and index.
  ISBN 978-1-61613-518-8
  1. Sotomayor, Sonia, 1954—Juvenile literature. 2. Hispanic American judges—Biography—Juvenile literature. 3. Judges— United States—Biography—Juvenile literature. I. Title.
  KF8745.S67G58 2011
  347.73'2634—dc22
  [B]
                                    2010000499

TABLE OF CONTENTS

Chapter 1	Controversial Call	6
Chapter 2	Young Sonia	16
Chapter 3	Princeton and Yale	26
Chapter 4	Launching Her Career	36
Chapter 5	Achieving Her Dream	46
Chapter 6	A New Nomination	54
Chapter 7	Supreme Court Justice Nomination	64
Chapter 8	The Confirmation Hearings	76
Chapter 9	Confirmed!	86
Timeline		96
Essential Facts		100
Additional Resources		102
Glossary		104
Source Notes		106
Index		110
About the Author		112

President Barack Obama's first nominee for the
U.S. Supreme Court was Sonia Sotomayor.

CONTROVERSIAL CALL

*I*n 2001, Sonia Sotomayor gave a speech
at the University of California, Berkeley.
During that speech, titled "In a Latina Judge's
Voice," Sotomayor stated that, as a judge, she could
no more disregard her upbringing as a Puerto Rican

girl in New York City than she could forget that she had two ears or two eyes. She challenged the idea that experiences, upbringing, and ethnicity play no part in the decision-making process of a judge. She acknowledged that her experiences as a woman and a minority definitely played an important role in handing down decisions from the bench. And she was not going to apologize for that.

Sotomayor seemed to invite criticism through controversial statements. For example, in the same speech she stated, "I would hope that a wise Latina woman with the richness of her experiences would more often than not reach a better conclusion than a white male who hasn't lived that life."[1] Later in that speech, she stated, "Whether born from experience or inherent physiological or cultural differences, our gender and national origin may and will make a difference in our judging."[2]

Critics interpreted her words as meaning she was more likely to rule in favor of minorities, like herself,

Judge Mario G. Olmos Memorial Lecture

The 2001 address Sotomayor gave at the University of California, Berkeley, was part of the School of Law's Honorable Mario G. Olmos Law & Cultural Diversity Memorial Lecture. The annual event is named for the Berkeley graduate who died in a car accident at the age of 43. After his death, the lecture series was established in his honor "to perpetuate the Judge's abiding commitment to the development of law promoting equality and justice for all people."[3]

than whites. They also took issue with what seemed to be a claim that a Hispanic woman would generally judge a case with greater equity than a white man would. Critics offered that a judge who held such ideas should not be considered for a seat on the U.S. Supreme Court.

Those same critics looked for a case in Sotomayor's body of work to exemplify these biases.

RICCI V. DESTEFANO

The case *Ricci v. DeStefano* involved a white firefighter named Frank Ricci. He was suing the mayor of New Haven, Connecticut, John DeStefano, for reverse racial discrimination. In other words, Ricci believed he had been discriminated against because he was white.

The case began when a group of New Haven firefighters took an exam evaluating their merit for a promotion. The city had worked hard to create an exam that would test firefighters fairly for promotions. Seventeen white applicants, including Ricci, passed the exam. But the African-American and Hispanic firefighters scored considerably lower than the whites. Only one of the minority applicants scored high enough to be considered for promotion.

Those who did not pass threatened to sue the city. In response, New Haven discarded the tests and did not promote any of the candidates who qualified. Because he passed the exam and was not promoted, Ricci sued for reverse discrimination.

Ricci lost the case in federal district court. He appealed the decision. This sent the case to the court of appeals, a higher court that has the power to uphold or overturn the lower, district court's ruling. The case was then heard by a panel of three judges: Sotomayor, Robert Sack, and Rosemary Pooler. The panel upheld the original ruling.

"We're not asking that unqualified people be hired—the city's not suggesting that. But if your test is going to always put a certain group at the bottom of the pass rate so they're never, ever going to be promoted, and there is a fair test that can be devised, then why shouldn't the city have an opportunity to try to look and see if it can develop that?"[4]

—*Sonia Sotomayor to the attorney representing Frank Ricci in* Ricci v. DeStefano

Some critics claimed that Sotomayor allowed favoritism toward minorities in the ruling. Some noted that she did not deem the case important enough because she did not publish an opinion—a written statement that explains the reasoning behind her judgment.

However, the way a court of appeal rules is complex. The judges do not hold another trial.

Sotomayor was a judge for a case filed by firefighter Frank Ricci.

In other words, they do not review evidence or
hear testimony from witnesses. Their job is only to
determine if the district court made an important
error. Sotomayor and the other judges decided that
the district court had not erred. So, the panel issued
its ruling as a summary order, a type of ruling that

does not include an opinion by any judge. Also, the decision was not Sotomayor's alone. The entire panel of judges—Sotomayor, Sack, and Pooler—ruled on the case.

AFFIRMATIVE ACTION

In *Ricci v. DeStefano*, Sotomayor was criticized for her perceived views regarding affirmative action. Affirmative action is a set of public policies enacted in the early 1960s and 1970s to ensure that minorities who had been discriminated against in the past would have a fair chance at employment. The legislation has been controversial. Many have argued that it is unfair to discriminate against one group of people to make up for past injustices to others. Some have claimed that the policy of affirmative action actually hurts minorities because their achievements will always be questioned.

Affirmative Action

Affirmative Action is a series of programs in the United States developed to create greater educational and employment opportunities for minorities and women. These programs were initially developed to help African Americans following decades of discrimination through state and local laws known as Jim Crow laws. For example, some laws required black children to attend different public schools than whites—schools that were not necessarily near their homes, were poorly or not maintained, and had only one toilet.

It has been argued that as a Latina, Sotomayor benefited from affirmative action. As she rose in her profession and earned appointments to more prestigious positions, some asserted that she was given preferential treatment because she is a Hispanic woman. Sotomayor has spoken of the legislation's influence on her life:

I am a product of affirmative action. I am the perfect affirmative action baby. I am Puerto Rican, born and raised in the south Bronx. My test scores were not comparable to my colleagues at Princeton and Yale. Not so far off so that I wasn't able to succeed at those institutions.[5]

Reversal for Ricci

Frank Ricci did not abandon his reverse discrimination case after Sotomayor, Sack, and Pooler ruled against him in 2008. Ricci's case made it as far as it could go in the U.S. justice system: the U.S. Supreme Court. The case was argued before the Court on April 22, 2009. The decision was handed down on June 29.

The Court reversed the ruling made by the court of appeals. The justices ruled, in a 5–4 vote, that Ricci and the other firefighters who passed the city's exam had been illegally denied promotions. When deciding the case, the justices considered Title VII of the 1964 Civil Rights Act, which bars discrimination in employment.

Justice Anthony Kennedy delivered the Court's decision, in which he explained that the city cannot simply throw out results of a test because it is afraid of being sued by some of the participants. Kennedy wrote,

Fear of litigation alone cannot justify an employer's reliance on race to the detriment of individuals who passed the examinations and qualified for promotions. The City's discarding the test results was impermissible under Title VII. . . .[6]

NOMINATING A SUPREME COURT JUSTICE

In 2009, President Barack Obama was given the opportunity to make his first nomination to the U.S. Supreme Court. Obama wanted his nominee to not only have professional credentials, but empathy— the ability and desire to put oneself in the hearts and minds of others. Obama wanted someone who understood the day-to-day lives of ordinary people. He wanted someone who would make informed rulings based on knowledge and experience. The president understood Sotomayor's philosophy of allowing her upbringing to play a role in making decisions from the bench. The president was criticized by those who believed the job of a Supreme Court justice was strictly the interpretation of the law. A senior member of Obama's staff countered that criticism by stating,

> What the president has said is that he is looking for someone who embodies legal excellence, restraint, a sense of how judging works and an understanding of its real-world consequences. If opponents want to say that only one of those is important, that is a debate we are willing to have.[7]

On May 26, 2009, that debate began when the first African-American president nominated the first Hispanic woman to the U.S. Supreme Court. If approved by the Senate Judiciary Committee and then the U.S. Senate, Sonia Sotomayor would become one of the nine judges serving on the highest court in the land.

"Throughout my seventeen years on the bench, I have witnessed the human consequences of my decisions. Those decisions have been made not to serve the interests of any one litigant, but always to serve the larger interest of impartial justice.

In the past month, many Senators have asked me about my judicial philosophy. It is simple: fidelity to the law. The task of a judge is not to make the law—it is to apply the law."[8]

—Sonia Sotomayor, opening statement before the Senate Judiciary Committee, July 13, 2009

Sotomayor's nomination by President Obama was the first step in her becoming a Supreme Court justice.

Sonia, age six or seven

YOUNG SONIA

Juan and Celina Sotomayor left their homeland of Puerto Rico during World War II (1941–1945). The couple moved to the United States, where they settled in the South Bronx neighborhood of New York City. The couple welcomed their first child, Sonia Maria, on June 25, 1954. Sonia's younger brother, Juan, was born two years later, in 1956.

Sonia's parents remained close to relatives on the island of Puerto Rico. The Sotomayors also had relatives in New York, who they often visited. Sonia's paternal grandmother lived in the Bronx, and the family would gather at her house to eat and play dominoes. During the summer, extended family would meet at nearby Orchard Beach to share each other's company and enjoy traditional Hispanic food.

During the 2001 speech at the University of California, Berkeley, Sotomayor explained her background and upbringing:

"Part of my Latina identity is the sound of merengue at all our family parties and the heart wrenching Spanish love songs that we enjoy. It is the memory of Saturday afternoon at the movies with my aunt and cousins. . . . My Latina soul was nourished as I visited and played at my grandmother's house with my cousins and extended family. They were my friends as I grew up. Being a Latina child was watching the adults playing dominos on Saturday night and us kids playing loteria, bingo, with my grandmother calling out the numbers which we marked on our cards with chick peas."[1]

—Sonia Sotomayor,
"A Latina Judge's Voice,"
University of California,
Berkeley, 2001

Who am I? I am a "Newyorkrican." For those of you on the West Coast who do not know what that term means: I am a born and bred New Yorker of Puerto Rican-born parents who came to the states during World War II.

Sonia lived at Bronxdale Houses as a child.

Like many other immigrants to this great land, my parents came because of poverty and to attempt to find and secure a better life for themselves and the family that they hoped to have. . . . The story of that success is what made me and what makes me the Latina that I am. The Latina side of my identity was forged and closely nurtured by my family through our shared experiences and traditions.

For me, a very special part of my being Latina is the mucho platos de arroz, gandules y pernil—rice, beans and pork—

that I have eaten at countless family holidays and special events. My Latina identity also includes, because of my particularly adventurous taste buds, morcilla—pig intestines, patitas de cerdo con garbanzo—pigs' feet with beans, and la lengua y orejas de cuchifrito—pigs' tongue and ears.[2]

While Sonia experienced her Puerto Rican heritage throughout her childhood, she was also exposed to people from a variety of backgrounds. She and her family moved to the Bronxdale Houses, a new housing development, in 1957. It was home to a mix of tenants, including Irish, Italians, Jews, Africans Americans, and Puerto Ricans.

Bronxdale was near Blessed Sacrament, the Catholic elementary school Sonia and Juan attended. While Sonia and her brother were busy at school, their parents were busy working. Sonia's father had the equivalent of a third-grade education and spoke only Spanish. He toiled as a tool-and-die worker in a factory. Sonia's mother was a homemaker.

As a young child, Sonia was faced with two difficult challenges. The first came when she was eight years old. Diagnosed with diabetes, Sonia required daily insulin injections. When she was nine years old, Sonia and her family suffered a tragic loss when her father died from heart problems. Sonia's mother was forced to raise her children alone.

She moved to a smaller apartment in the housing development where the family had been living. The apartment overlooked Blessed Sacrament, and Celina would often look for her children when they were outside with their classmates.

Celina took a job as a nurse, working six days a week to support herself, Sonia, and young Juan. Sonia drew great inspiration from her mother's work

---

Bronxdale Houses

Bronxdale Houses is a large housing development of 28 buildings with a total of 1,496 apartments. The development was new when the Sotomayors moved there in the late 1950s. Most Bronxdale residents were working class. Approximately 10 percent were on welfare.

Today, Bronxdale is very different. *Washington Post* reporter Robin Shulman wrote about the development in late spring 2009. Shulman interviewed Taur Orange, one of the Sotomayors' former neighbors:

Walk through the red-brick buildings of Bronxdale Houses . . . and find broken elevators; smashed windows, lights and front-door locks; and hallways that stink of urine. . . . It's the kind of place where people fight and no one bothers to call the cops. . . . Taur Orange . . . visited there after leaving for college, and found the Houses transformed.

Graffiti covered the walls. People feared their neighbors. Most horrifyingly, she said, was finding people she had grown up with losing themselves in drugs. . . . "I would come home and get updates from people whose lives had just turned. You began to hear about some childhood friends who had died of overdoses."[3]

ethic. Sonia also admired how her mother embraced her role as the emotional and spiritual leader of the family.

Celina regularly repeated to Sonia and her brother, "I don't care what you do, but be the best at it."[4] These words served as a constant reminder to Sonia that she needed to work hard to achieve her goals and overcome any challenges she faced.

EDUCATION FIRST

Celina insisted that her children take learning seriously. She was the only parent in their neighborhood to purchase encyclopedias. Sonia's mother was adamant about making the most out of the educational opportunities presented to Sonia and Juan. She spent much of her pay to send Sonia and Juan to a private Catholic school.

The thirst for knowledge and motivation to forge a bright future

Diabetes

Diabetes has two forms: type I and type II. Both diseases have to do with the body's ability to use glucose, a type of sugar used as fuel. The difference in the types of diabetes pertains to why the blood sugar gets too high. Sonia has type I diabetes. Her pancreas does not make the insulin her body needs to help cells absorb glucose, so she must inject insulin into her body. Only 5 to 10 percent of all diabetes cases are type I and require insulin. Type I diabetes is also called juvenile diabetes because it is usually diagnosed in very young people.

Sonia attended Blessed Sacrament Church and School.

marked Sonia's childhood. She was influenced by
books and television. She enjoyed reading books
about Nancy Drew, a girl detective who liked to solve
mysteries. Inspired by the character, Sonia wanted
to become a detective, but she gave up that dream
due to her diabetes. She was told that a less stressful
and physically demanding career would be better for
her health.

But Sonia soon found another career to aspire to. She began watching a popular television program. *Perry Mason* was a court drama in which the title character, the lawyer Perry Mason, helped solve crimes. One particular episode sparked Sonia's interest in pursuing law. She explained what happened in that story line that had such a strong effect on her:

Perry Mason

Sonia spoke about the episode of *Perry Mason* that had such a strong effect on her: "I thought, what a wonderful occupation to have. And I made the quantum leap: If that was the prosecutor's job, then the guy who made the decision to dismiss the case was the judge. That was what I was going to be."[6]

In one of the episodes, at the end of the episode, Perry Mason, with the character who played the prosecutor in the case, were meeting up after the case, and Perry said to the prosecutor: "It must cause you some pain, having expended all that effort in your case, to have the charges dismissed." And the prosecutor looked up and said: "No, my job as a prosecutor is to do justice, and justice is served when a guilty man is convicted and when an innocent man is not."[5]

A NEW HOME

When Sonia was growing up, Bronxdale Houses was a newer, well-kept community. In order to rent, a tenant was required to have a job and no history of drug addiction. But communities often change with time, and Bronxdale was no exception. During the late 1960s and early 1970s, addiction to hard drugs became a way of life for many young people in New York City. Those who made dangerous choices frightened Celina Sotomayor. In 1970, during her daughter's sophomore year in high school, she moved her family north in the Bronx to a new and safer development.

Juan Sotomayor

The emphasis Celina Sotomayor put on education influenced both of her children. While Sonia became successful in the field of law, Juan pursued medicine. He earned a medical degree from New York University in 1981 and later opened his own practice as an allergist in Syracuse, New York.

Although the family moved, Sonia and Juan continued to attend Cardinal Spellman High School. An active student, Sonia became involved in activities geared toward forging a law career. She was elected to student government and was a member of its forensics team, which required her to give long speeches.

Sonia graduated from Cardinal Spellman in 1972. At the top of her class academically, she was named valedictorian. Sonia Sotomayor was on her way to college. ―

Sonia's eighth grade graduation photograph

Sonia Sotomayor in a Princeton University yearbook photograph

PRINCETON AND YALE

In 1972, Sotomayor moved to New Jersey
to attend Princeton University. She began
a new—and very different—phase in her life.
Sotomayor's background was different from
her peers' backgrounds. The majority of her fellow

students came from far wealthier families and had been educated at elite private schools. Sotomayor was one of the fortunate beneficiaries of a minority recruiting drive that brought underprivileged students to Princeton. Such campaigns to improve opportunities for minority students in the United States had become common by the early 1970s.

CHALLENGES AT PRINCETON

Although she was attending one of the nation's top universities, 18-year-old Sotomayor did not feel fortunate. She felt so out of place in the classroom that she did not raise her hand to contribute to discussions. She asked no questions because she was afraid of embarrassing herself. And, to her dismay, Sotomayor learned that she was woefully lacking in writing skills, which she worked hard to improve.

Yankees Fan

Sotomayor is a passionate fan of the most successful sports franchise in U.S. history.

She was raised to be and remains a die-hard fan of the New York Yankees. She grew up in the Bronx near Yankee Stadium and followed her favorite baseball team as it won many World Series championships.

"With most students, the time I spent marking up papers was largely wasted. But Sonia took the comments seriously. She sought me out to go over her essays. In each paper, I would focus on a different shortcoming: Spanglish, tenses, passive voice. Taking such constant criticism could not have been easy, but Sonia kept coming back. She even read grammar books during her summer breaks. . . . Years later, she told me that she was particularly proud of how the second reader of her thesis . . . had told her it was the best-written senior thesis he had read."[1]

—Peter Winn, *Sotomayor's mentor at Princeton*

She struggled socially as well. She did not fit in with most of the other students, who were almost entirely white men. Sotomayor gained comfort in the company of the few other minority students. She joined the Third World Center group, where she met students with backgrounds similar to her own. They discussed and became involved in politics. The students also shared their experiences at Princeton and talked about their personal lives, which helped them to feel less isolated.

Blossoming Young Woman

Despite the challenges she faced, Sotomayor still performed exceptionally well academically. With time, Sotomayor's confidence grew. Initially, she was hesitant to join a group of Puerto Rican campus activists, but when she did, Sotomayor made her mark. In 1974,

Sotomayor attended Princeton University, a prestigious Ivy League school located in New Jersey.

she and other students filed a complaint with the U.S. Department of Health, Education, and Welfare alleging Princeton University's lack of commitment to bringing minority students and faculty into the school. The complaint quickly sparked a debate at Princeton and other universities about how to better diversify its student populations.

By her senior year, Sotomayor had gone from being a wallflower to a school leader. In 1976, she was awarded the M. Taylor Pyne Honor Prize. Given annually to one or more seniors who excelled academically and in extracurricular work, it is the highest honor a Princeton student can receive from the university. That spring, Sotomayor graduated with top honors—summa cum laude—with a degree in history.

Sotomayor experienced another major life event a few months later. She wed Kevin Edward Noonan in August. The couple had been dating since high school. Soon after the wedding, she enrolled at Yale Law School in New Haven, Connecticut.

The Pyne Prize

Sotomayor was one of two Princeton seniors to receive the M. Taylor Pyne Honor Prize in 1976, the highest honor a Princeton student can receive. The annual award is named for Moses Taylor Pyne, who graduated from Princeton in 1877. The prize is "awarded to the senior who has most clearly manifested excellent scholarship, strength of character and effective leadership."[2]

The other recipient was J. David Germany, an economics major. The prize included $3,900, the cost of one year of tuition in 1976. Sotomayor and Germany shared the money.

The February 28, 1976, issue of Princeton's newspaper, the *Daily Princetonian*, included an article in which Adam Gilinsky, wrote,

Sotomayor, a history major, has maintained almost straight A's for the last two years, but is especially known for her extracurricular activities.

Her dedication to the life of minority students at Princeton has been illustrated by her service on the Governance Board of the Third World Center and in her efforts to form the Latino Students Organization.

She also has worked as a volunteer at Trenton Psychiatric Hospital and has served on the student-faculty Discipline Committee.[3]

GAINING A REPUTATION

In law school, Sotomayor faced studies even more challenging than those at Princeton. She continued to display the self-assurance she had gained while an undergraduate student. Yale classmate Robert Klonoff recalled of Sotomayor,

> She was always willing to speak up and give her point of view. I just remember, even back then, thinking that in a group of very, very smart people she was destined to go to great places.[4]

Sotomayor gained a reputation for never using her background as a crutch. Stephen Carter, another Yale classmate, said,

> She would never sit around and say, "Oh well, I grew up in a housing project so I know." She didn't feel her background gave her some kind of [advantage in an argument]. She wanted the argument to work. She would tell you why she thought something, and the "why" never had anything to do with where she came from.[5]

Sotomayor excelled academically at Yale and had the distinction of serving as editor of the *Yale Law Journal*. She also became increasingly involved in extracurricular activities. Sotomayor impressed students and law professors with her ability to think through a problem fairly and without bias.

She understood that every argument had a certain amount of uncertainty to consider—evidence from both sides of a case is never perfectly clear. Carter noticed Sotomayor's ability to weigh evidence. He praised her,

> She looks and she says, "I understand a lot of people think A, and a lot of people Z, but if you look at this carefully the real answer is somewhere between those." And indeed what she does in finding these in-between answers is she applies a practical sense, the sense of someone who has been a courtroom lawyer.[6]

Sotomayor became known as someone who fought against discrimination, and this reputation extended beyond Yale. In 1978, during her final year of law school, she grabbed national headlines after a recruiting dinner with a Washington DC law firm. A representative of Shaw, Pittman, Potts & Trowbridge

Yale Law Journal

While she was a law student at Yale University, Sotomayor served as editor of the *Yale Law Journal*. Founded in 1891, the journal is published eight times a year and includes articles, book reviews, and essays by scholars and students. The journal is well-known and well-cited by those in the legal discipline. Other Supreme Court justices who have held the prestigious role of editor of the *Yale Law Journal* include Abe Fortas and Samuel Alito.

When she was a student at Yale, Sotomayor spent
her time studying U.S. legislation.

asked Sotomayor what she felt were offensive
questions. He asked if firms should hire minority
students with weaker credentials only to fire them in
a few years. Sotomayor was also asked if she would
have been admitted to the Yale Law School if she had
not been Puerto Rican.

Upset about the questions, she confronted the
recruiter the next day at her job interview. He was
surprised to learn of her anger and offered her an
opportunity to attend more interviews. Instead, she

Measuring Up

Some would argue that the law firm recruiter who offended Sotomayor was not acting out of prejudice or discrimination. Sotomayor admitted that her own feeling of being an outsider at Princeton and Yale played a role in her reaction. She commented later that such discomfort remained with her for years thereafter: "I have spent my years since Princeton, while at law school and in my various professional jobs, not feeling a part of the worlds I inhabit. I am always looking over my shoulder wondering if I measure up."[7]

along with a group of Yale student teachers filed a formal complaint against the law firm, requesting an official apology. The group received an apology that the members considered insincere. A second apology was offered that the group found satisfactory. Sotomayor's influence was clear—the law firm was nearly barred from recruiting at Yale.

In 1979, Sotomayor graduated from Yale with a law degree. She would soon begin her career in law, displaying her knowledge and abilities in the working world. ⌐

Yale University, where Sotomayor received her law degree

*After receiving her law degree, Sotomayor
returned to New York City.*

LAUNCHING HER CAREER

fter completing her law degree and
passing the bar exam in 1980, Sonia
Sotomayor was officially a lawyer. She was also ready
and eager to pursue a career in law. She made a
promising start when she was hired as an assistant

district attorney in Manhattan. Sotomayor was back in her hometown of New York City working at Trial Bureau 50.

The district attorney is the public official who represents the government in prosecuting criminal cases. Sotomayor joined the district attorney's office during a major crime wave. Rival gangs battled over territory. People were mugged, burglarized, or beaten.

The young attorney's caseload ranged from 60 to 80 cases at a time. Her work included investigating and evaluating the cases and making presentations to grand juries. A grand jury is a group of citizens assigned the task of determining whether a person should be officially charged with a crime. In addition, Sotomayor wrote briefs and arguments, legal documentation required as part of her trial work. As a part of her trial work, she also

Personal Interests

While Sotomayor is a dedicated worker, she also enjoys her personal time. She likes vacationing abroad, relaxing in spas, and attending craft fairs. Sotomayor also loves to dance.

questioned witnesses and even moved jury members to tears on occasion. Her interrogation skills impressed fellow attorneys in court.

QUICKLY PROMOTED

Sotomayor's overwhelming workload meant long hours at the office. She was often seen chugging cans of diet soda to keep awake and attentive. But the 12-hour-a-day job prepared her well for higher callings. Her boss, Warren Murray, later stated, "If you can handle a felony case load in New York County, you can run a small country."[1]

After a short period of time handling minor cases, Sotomayor's talent became apparent. She was quickly promoted to prosecute some of the many murder cases handled by the bureau. With more than 1,800 homicides in New York City in 1979, Sotomayor and the other state attorneys were busy.

Sotomayor the Standout

As a district attorney, Sotomayor forged a life-long friendship while working on her second trial. She met Dawn Cardi, another rookie lawyer. Cardi recalled being quite impressed with Sotomayor. "She's really, really smart and very well prepared," Cardi said. "She was an excellent trial attorney. She had a talent for it. Did anybody think she was going to the Supreme Court? Of course not. But when you look back, you see she always stood out. She was always really a cut above."[2]

Sotomayor spent much of her time on the streets with police to find witnesses and gather evidence. The streets were far more violent than what she had known growing up. Drug dealing and gang warfare led to violent crime, including murder. Sotomayor tried to gather information from people such as drug addicts and gang members in the toughest slums in town.

TRYING THE TARZAN BURGLAR

One of Sotomayor's more dangerous cases was prosecuting what became

The Bar Exam

Graduating from law school is not enough to become a lawyer in the United States. One must pass the bar exam, a government-issued law test, to practice law legally.

There are several versions of the bar exam. Each U.S. state and territory has its own bar exam that addresses the laws specific to that state or territory. A law student must pass a particular state's exam to practice law in that state.

Though the exam questions vary by state, bar exams have a common format: essay questions. The exams are lengthy and often take one or two days to complete. In addition, depending on the state, test takers may take the multistate bar exam, which requires an additional day of testing. This exam has 200 questions about common law.

States vary in what they offer for a bar exam. For example, Louisiana does not offer the multistate bar exam. This is because common law does not apply to Louisiana. California's bar exam includes the California Performance Test in which test takers have three hours to take in and respond to a fictional case with a memorandum and an opinion or finding.

Preparing for the bar exam, regardless of state, requires a lot of time and dedication. Many students attend test-prep classes. Once a student passes the bar exam, he or she is admitted to the Bar Association.

While working for the district attorney's office, Sotomayor often worked with police officers to send criminals to jail.

known as the Tarzan Burglar case. Richard Maddicks burglarized apartments, robbed residents at gunpoint, and murdered those who tried to stop him. He used ropes and cables to swing from building to building, earning him the nickname Tarzan.

In the Tarzan Burglar case, Maddicks was accused of robbing and subsequently killing several individuals, including one with a gunshot to the head. While working on the case, Sotomayor accompanied detectives into dangerous tenements inhabited by drug dealers and drug addicts. Her efforts were rewarded. She secured important testimony from Maddicks's girlfriend and one of his neighbors.

Sotomayor played a significant role in prosecuting the case. She helped write the opening statement of the lead prosecuting attorney. She created a large chart that depicted a pattern to Maddicks's crimes that was shown during the trial. Sotomayor also took on the important role of questioning 20 witnesses. She played upon the emotions of jury members to prove her case, bringing some to tears as she questioned the girlfriend of a man Maddicks had allegedly killed.

The trial lasted five weeks. Sotomayor's hard work paid off when Maddicks was convicted of murder, robbery, and other crimes. He was sentenced to more than 60 years in prison. Lead prosecutor Hugh H. Mo was impressed with Sotomayor's work. "She was very focused, very ambitious, very competent, very hardworking," he said. "She wanted to reach the highest pinnacle of the profession and

Origin of the Bar

The *bar* in bar exam refers to the actual wooden bar in the courtroom that separates the lawyers, judge, and other court officials from those simply attending court—the audience.

didn't think that was far-fetched. You could see it. She wanted to make history."[3]

LIFE CHANGES

In 1983, Sotomayor's personal life changed. She and her husband, Kevin Noonan, divorced. The following year, her professional life changed as well.

Sotomayor wanted to make more money, so she decided to work in the private sector. Pavia & Harcourt, a private law firm in Manhattan, had been courting her with job offers. In 1984, she joined the small company at the entry level for a lawyer: an associate.

Her work at Pavia & Harcourt was far different from what she had known. Rather than dealing with criminals, Sotomayor tackled commercial cases on behalf of clients such as handbag manufacturer Fendi and automakers Fiat and Ferrari.

Pavia & Harcourt

The law firm Pavia & Harcourt was founded in 1940 to represent Italian companies in the United States. Most of the companies specialized in the fashion industry. The firm still works with European manufacturers and takes pride in the fact that its attorneys are fluent in languages such as Italian, French, Spanish, and Portuguese. Pavia & Harcourt is based on Madison Avenue in New York City and also has offices in Paris, France, and Milan, Italy.

Family has always been important to Sotomayor, pictured with her niece.

She enjoyed her greater salary, but she missed the action of her previous job. She was eager to be assigned projects that would require tasks similar to those of the district attorney's office, and she promptly got to work when such opportunities arose. On one occasion, Sotomayor accompanied a police raid of a counterfeiting business in Harlem, one of the city's many neighborhoods. Former coworker Steven Skulnik recalled it vividly,

I was crouched in the van, waiting for things to clear up, and Sonia goes running out with the investigators. She got a thrill out of the cops and robbers stuff. It's not something you expect to see from a corporate attorney.[4]

Sotomayor & Associates

From the years 1983 to 1986, Sotomayor had a consulting business: Sotomayor & Associates. She ran the business from her home during the time she worked for the district attorney and then for Pavia & Harcourt. Sotomayor has explained of her business that she aided "family and friends in their real estate, business and estate planning decisions" and when clients "required more substantial legal representation, I referred the matter to my firm, Pavia & Harcourt, or to others with appropriate expertise."[5]

Sotomayor's performance at Pavia & Harcourt was so impressive that she eventually became a partner in the firm. Other lawyers might have wanted to stay after such a promotion, but Sotomayor yearned to work on cases that had a greater impact on the lives of ordinary people. She wanted to realize her childhood dream of becoming a judge. However, unlike most jobs, one cannot submit an application to be a judge. Depending on the state, judges are appointed or elected. In New York, Sotomayor would have to continue to work hard as an attorney, hoping an official who could place her in her dream role would take notice.

Sotomayor spent a lot of time in court while working as a lawyer.

*Following years of dedication to her work as an attorney,
Sotomayor was nominated to become a judge.*

ACHIEVING HER DREAM

*M*any lawyers would have been quite
content with the job Sonia Sotomayor
had as an attorney with the New York City law firm
Pavia & Harcourt. She worked on the twelfth floor of
a bright, cheery office that offered a beautiful view of

Manhattan. And her paycheck would have satisfied most young lawyers.

But Sotomayor wanted more than a nice office and money. She wanted to be more than an attorney— she aspired to use her knowledge and experience in other ways. Sotomayor's thoughts returned to *Perry Mason,* the show that had inspired her to seek a career as a judge when she was young.

Sotomayor worked for Pavia & Harcourt for eight years, from 1984 to 1992. During that time, she had caught the attention of New York Senator Daniel Patrick Moynihan. Impressed with the young woman's work, he recommended to President George H. W. Bush that she be nominated to the U.S. District Court for the Southern District of New York. This district covered two New York City boroughs—Manhattan and the Bronx—and six counties north of New York City.

"I've gotten letters from people who remember me in grammar school saying that this is what I wanted."[1]

—*Sonia Sotomayor in response to being confirmed a judge*

Bush was a Republican, and Sotomayor was a Democrat. However, he did not let this difference influence his nomination of Sotomayor, now 37 years old, in November 1991. The Senate Judiciary Committee confirmed the nomination in June 1992. Sotomayor's childhood dream had been realized—she was now a judge.

A Champion of Freedoms

Right away, Sotomayor gained a reputation as a judge who would champion the freedoms outlined by the Bill of Rights. These included freedom of the press, freedom of expression, and freedom of assembly. The new judge was presented a difficult case in January 1993 after former White House Counsel Vincent Foster committed suicide. He left a suicide note, which had been torn up. The government refused to release a copy of the note, citing privacy considerations for Foster's family. But Sotomayor ordered that the suicide note be released to the *Wall Street Journal*. The ruling was applauded as standing up for the freedom of the press.

In September of that year, she ruled in favor of freedom of assembly. The government had tried to seize a New York building owned by the Hell's

Angels motorcycle club, claiming that it was a center of drug dealing. It was also alleged that the building promoted other criminal activity. Sotomayor ruled that the government had insufficient evidence for its claims. The Hell's Angels were allowed to remain in the building.

A few months later, she was embraced as an advocate of freedom of expression when she reversed a law in the town of White Plains, New York. That law banned the public showing

Becoming a Federal Judge

Federal judges hear cases that deal with federal, as opposed to state, laws—laws enacted by the U.S. Congress. The U.S. federal court system has three main levels. The district courts are at the bottom. These are trial courts that review evidence and hear testimony. The courts of appeals are next. These higher courts can overrule a district court ruling. At the top is the Supreme Court.

Each district court serves its own region. Some states have one district court; some have several. The United States has 94 district courts. In turn, several districts comprise a federal circuit. There are 12 regional circuits; each is served by its own court of appeals. A thirteenth circuit serves the entire United States, but in a limited way. The Court of Appeals for the Federal Circuit has nationwide jurisdiction over specialized cases, including cases regarding patents and trademarks.

The Supreme Court decides cases originating throughout the United States. The court has varied in size, ranging from 5 to 10 justices. Currently, there are 9 Supreme Court justices.

As outlined in the U.S. Constitution, federal judges are nominated by the president and confirmed by the U.S. Senate. Usually, the Senate Judiciary Committee holds a confirmation hearing for each nominee. Federal judges are appointed to life terms.

of religious or political symbols
in city parks.

THE BASEBALL STRIKE

Sotomayor became well-known
notoriety as a district court judge in
1995 when she ended a strike in the
sport she loved: baseball. Professional
baseball players walked out during the
1994 season of Major League Baseball
(MLB). The MLB team owners and
the players' union could not agree on
salary guidelines. The owners wanted
to limit the amount of money players
could receive, but the players rejected
the salary cap, claiming it would
mean less money for the players. In
turn, owners limited players' ability
to negotiate their salaries.

The sport was at a standstill.
In 1994, for the first time in
MLB history, the World Series was
cancelled. Fans were irate. So were
the members of Congress who had
introduced several bills in a frantic

1995 World Series

Once the 1995 baseball
strike ended, MLB play-
ers eagerly returned to
the sport they loved. The
season was shorter than
usual, but it was com-
pleted in its usual fashion:
with the World Series.
That year, the Atlanta
Braves defeated the
Cleveland Indians 4–2 in
the series.

attempt to end the strike. President
Bill Clinton ordered the two sides
to work out their differences by
February 6, 1995. The deadline was
just weeks before spring training was
scheduled to begin. Resolving the
issue by the February deadline would
mean that professional baseball would
proceed as usual.

That deadline passed with no
agreement. In March, with the threat
of another baseball season being
lost, the dispute was handed over to
Sotomayor. After only 15 minutes of
listening to the evidence, Sotomayor
granted an injunction against the
owners, forcing them to agree to
return to the way things were before
the salary caps.

The fans and most players were
ecstatic, but the owners were not
happy. They challenged Sotomayor's
ruling. But the ruling was upheld by
the U.S. Court of Appeals for the
Second Circuit. The 1995 season was

Praise for Taking Action

More than a decade after
her role in the baseball
strike, Major League
Baseball Players Asso-
ciation Executive Director
Donald Fehr praised
Sotomayor for taking
action. Fehr said, "Her
ruling did not produce
an agreement, but it gave
the parties time to get on
with normal business and
get back to the bargain-
ing table and produce
an agreement. If it hadn't
ended when she ended it,
it would have gone on for
some time and it would
have gotten uglier and
uglier."[2]

Ruling in Favor of the Homeless

Sotomayor continued to establish herself as a capable judge in March 1998. A case revolved around two nonprofit organizations that had been recruiting home-less people to work for as little as one dollar an hour in return for what was claimed to be job training. She ruled the practice illegal and forced the organizations to pay the 198 homeless people a total of $816,000. They received their payments in 2000.

delayed for a short time. Once play resumed, the season went on as usual, but with fewer games because of the late start.

Sotomayor's speedy ruling brought both praise and criticism. It gave the two sides an opportunity to work out an agreement—which they did in November 1996—while still giving the fans baseball.

Her work for the U.S. District Court for the Southern District of New York did not go unnoticed. In a few years, she would be nominated by a different president to a new judicial position.

After Sotomayor helped end the baseball strike in 1995, New York Yankees fans promptly bought tickets to attend a game.

President Bill Clinton recognized Sotomayor's skills as a judge when he nominated her to the U.S. Court of Appeals for the Second Circuit.

A NEW NOMINATION

onfirmation hearings can be intense for high-level federal judicial seats, as so much is at stake. For one, federal rulings can have far-reaching impact. Also, the judges are appointed for life, which means they will likely hold their positions for many years or even decades.

Candidates for federal judgeships are nominated by the president and confirmed by the Senate. That means that a nominee must pass intense scrutiny by Senate members. They examine his or her rulings in earlier cases for a hint at what may be in store. For example, if a nominee ruled a particular way on a topic, people might assume the nominee will rule similarly in the future. Senators who do not agree with how a prospective judge may vote on certain issues will fight to prevent or delay the candidate's confirmation.

This was the case when Democratic president Bill Clinton nominated Sonia Sotomayor to the U.S. Court of Appeals for the Second Circuit in June 1997. Conservative Republicans tried to block her confirmation, contending that Sotomayor would favor Hispanics and other minorities in her decisions.

The Two-Party System

In proceedings such as judicial confirmations, politicians often vote along party lines. The United States has a two-party system of politics. In this system, citizens vote for representatives who are affiliated with one of the two major parties. In Congress, the party that has the most representatives holds the majority and has greater power in making policy and controlling the business of that body. Since the 1860s, these two parties have been the Republicans and Democrats in the United States. Most elected officials belong to one of these parties. There are other political parties in the United States. Sometimes, candidates from these third parties do influence elections by taking votes from one of the major party candidates.

Some critics claimed Sotomayor was a judicial activist, a judge who rules based on personal or political beliefs rather than solely on an interpretation of the law itself. Sotomayor's opponents also feared Sotomayor would support the current law on abortion as it came up in future cases. As a member of the nation's highest court, her opinion about abortion would affect millions of Americans. Sotomayor's critics also wanted to block her now, knowing that this

---

Other Constitutional Cases

In addition to ruling on cases involving First Amendment rights—freedoms of the press, expression, and assembly—Sotomayor has heard cases that address other constitutional amendments. Several of her cases have involved the Eighth Amendment. Some prisoners believed they were receiving treatment that was cruel and unusual because it was deliberately indifferent.

The Eighth Amendment prohibits the federal government from imposing excessive bail, excessive fines, or cruel and unusual punishment. In 1997, Sotomayor ruled on *Holton v. Fraitellone*. The case involved a prison inmate suing the prison's oral surgeon for lack of care for a painful jaw condition. The doctor neither took X-rays of the prisoner nor performed surgery, even though ten other doctors recommended the procedure. Sotomayor determined that the oral surgeon showed deliberate indifference and ruled in favor of the inmate.

That same year, Sotomayor ruled in *Vento v. Lord*, a case in which an inmate claimed that she did not receive proper X-rays. In this case, Sotomayor ruled against the prisoner, determining that the woman was not a victim of deliberate indifference. Rather, Sotomayor concluded that the prisoner disagreed with the medical diagnosis she received and was unhappy with her medical treatment.

appointment would put her in line to be nominated later to the Supreme Court.

Sotomayor's opponents stalled the confirmation process. Democratic senator Patrick Leahy of Vermont was angered by this. He stated that the Republicans who continued to delay debate were doing so for underhanded reasons:

> The reasons are stupid at best and cowardly at worst. What they are saying is that they have a brilliant judge who also happens to be a woman and Hispanic, and they haven't got the guts to stand up and argue publicly against her on the (Senate) floor. They just want to hide in their cloakrooms and do her in quietly.[1]

Conservatives succeeded in creating roadblocks that delayed the nomination hearing for months, but they failed to keep Sotomayor from being appointed. The Senate Judiciary Committee overwhelmingly approved Sotomayor's nomination in March 1998. She was approved in the Senate by a landslide 68–28 vote.

Pappas v. Giuliani

Following her appointment to the U.S. Court of Appeals for the Second Circuit, Sotomayor showed

The judge finalizes rulings in court with the banging of a gavel.

many critics that she could follow the law exactly in cases involving racial discrimination and abortion. The 2002 case *Pappas v. Giuliani* centered on a police officer, Thomas Pappas, who had been fired by the New York City Police Department. Pappas had been caught sending anonymous hate mail from his home. He wrote the racist letters to political organizations that had asked him for donations.

The final court ruling found that the police department was justified in dismissing Pappas. However, Sotomayor did not agree with the majority that he should have been fired. She wrote in her dissenting opinion that the material Pappas distributed was offensive and hateful, but he had sent it as a private citizen and not as a public employee. Therefore, it fell into the category of freedom of speech.

CENTER FOR REPRODUCTIVE LAW AND POLICY V. BUSH

The U.S. Court of Appeals for the Second Circuit also heard an abortion case in 2002. In *Center for Reproductive Law and Policy v. Bush*, Sotomayor ruled against an abortion-rights group that challenged a policy of President George W. Bush. The policy stated that an overseas organization that received money from the United States could neither

"I am reminded each day that I render decisions that affect people concretely and that I owe them constant and complete vigilance in checking my assumptions, presumptions and perspectives and . . . reevaluate them and change as circumstances and cases before me requires. I can and do aspire to be greater than the sum total of my experiences but I accept my limitations. I willingly accept that we who judge must not deny the differences resulting from experience and heritage but attempt, as the Supreme Court suggests, continuously to judge when those opinions, sympathies and prejudices are appropriate."[2]

—Sonia Sotomayor,
"A Latina Judge's Voice,"
University of California,
Berkeley, 2001

promote nor perform abortions. As part of the panel of three judges ruling on the case, Sotomayor upheld the Bush administration's decision, which was antiabortion.

This ruling may have swayed beliefs regarding Sotomayor's stance on abortion. However, rather than basing the ruling on a personal view, Sotomayor drew from precedent, or previous court decisions on similar cases, to reach her decision.

"There is a reason why the statue of Justice wears a blindfold. There are things that courts are not supposed to see or recognize when making their decisions—the race you belong to, whether you are rich or poor, and other personal things that could bias decisions by judges or juries."[3]

—Thomas Sowell, "The Statue of Justice Wears a Blindfold"

Doninger v. Niehoff

In *Pappas v. Giuliani*, Sotomayor had ruled in favor of freedoms of speech and expression. But in other rulings, including a March 2008 decision regarding the rights of a Connecticut high school student, she showed that she could land on the other side of the issue.

Avery Doninger had posted negative comments about school administrators on the Internet.

School officials learned of Doninger's online commentary and banned her from participating in school government. The court case focused on the issue of whether Doninger's freedom of speech off school grounds could be limited.

Sotomayor and two other judges ruled that what Doninger had written in her blog would be disruptive to the school and that the disciplinary action should stand. They also decided that it was not their place to determine whether the school's action was wise, acknowledging that perhaps the administrators had been too harsh in dealing with the student.

Sotomayor was criticized by some after the ruling in *Doninger v. Niehoff*. Jonathan Turley, a law professor at George Washington University, claimed that the student's First Amendment right to freedom of speech had been violated and that Sotomayor had upheld that violation.

Fast Track to the Highest Court?

Critics of the Republicans who stalled the confirmation process were puzzled by why some believed Sotomayor was on a speedy path to the Supreme Court. Though Hispanic groups had been urging President Clinton to nominate the first Hispanic justice to the nation's highest court, officials in his administration had made no commitment to doing so.

In addition, the Hispanic National Bar Association, which represents Hispanic lawyers and judges, had submitted a list of potential candidates to the Supreme Court that did not include Sotomayor.

He also claimed that students are taught a bad lesson about democracy when they are prevented from speaking out. "The continual expansion of the authority of school officials over student speeches teaches a foul lesson to these future citizens," Turley stated.[4]

By that time, Sotomayor had become accustomed to negative comments directed at her by the media and others. But those would not compare to the flood of criticism she would soon receive. Sotomayor's work had been noticed, and she was on her way to another nomination. This time, Sotomayor would hold her ground as she took part in the confirmation hearings for a spot on the nation's highest court. ⌒

Sotomayor in her New York City office when she served on
the U.S. Court of Appeals for the Second Circuit

The U.S. political situation changed dramatically with the 2008 election.

SUPREME COURT JUSTICE NOMINATION

Sonia Sotomayor served on the U.S. Court of Appeals for the Second Circuit during the early 2000s. During this time, the U.S. political landscape changed drastically. George W. Bush was elected president in 2000 and won reelection in 2004. But by the middle of his second term in office, many Americans had grown unhappy with the president and the Republican Party. His approval ratings plummeted due to an unpopular war in Iraq and a struggling economy.

THE HISPANIC VOTE IN 2008

One group with which Bush and the Republicans lost popularity was the Hispanic-American population. Hispanic Americans turned away from the Republicans in the November 2008 elections. Republican presidential candidate John McCain received far less support from Hispanic voters than had previous candidates from his party. The younger generation of Hispanics had embraced the Democrats, particularly the ideas of presidential nominee Barack Obama.

Obama successfully lured the Hispanic-American vote during his campaign. The group voted overwhelmingly in his favor on election day, with 14 percent more Hispanics turning out to vote than in the previous presidential election. Colorado, Florida, and New Mexico were the three battleground states where the Democrats and Obama made big gains. Nationwide, Hispanic Americans voted for Obama by a margin of more than 2–1, and nearly 80 percent of young Hispanic-American voters cast their ballots for the Democrat.

NOMINATED!

Obama realized that the Hispanic population was beginning to play a larger part than before in shaping politics in the United States. He may have believed that perhaps it was time they were represented on the country's highest court.

Before Obama was even sworn into office on January 20, 2009, he had created a list of possible

Hispanic Americans

According to the Pew Hispanic Center, the total Hispanic-American population was just more than 45 million in 2009, which is approximately 15 percent of the entire population of the United States. There are nearly 30 million Mexican Americans, the largest Hispanic population in the nation. Pew reported that those of Puerto Rican descent represent the second-largest Hispanic population in the United States. Puerto Ricans have had U.S. citizenship since 1917. As of early 2010, more than 4 million Puerto Ricans are U.S. citizens.

nominees. Obama had not expected to need the list soon, but Justice Ruth Bader Ginsburg underwent surgery in February for pancreatic cancer. This type of cancer is one of the most lethal. Fortunately, the surgery resulted in a good prognosis for Ginsburg, and she continued to serve in her role as a justice. However, on April 30, Justice David Souter announced that he would retire at the end of the Court's 2008–2009 term.

President Obama, left, and Sotomayor

At first, Obama's list had more than three dozen names. That number was cut down significantly by the middle of May, when only four names remained: Elena Kagan, Janet Napolitano, Diane Wood, and Sotomayor. Kagan had been named solicitor general of the United States in March, a role in which she represented the United States in Supreme Court cases. Napolitano was the head of the Department of

Homeland Security. Wood and Sotomayor were both serving as judges.

The president met with each of the four candidates. He knew Kagan, Napolitano, and Wood personally, but not Sotomayor. Before meeting with the president for about an hour on May 21,

Sotomayor also met with members of the White House staff.

Obama had a decision the next day, but he was not 100 percent certain about his choice. He wanted the weekend to think about his choice for nominee. In the meantime, Vice President Joe Biden called Sotomayor. Following that conversation, Sotomayor revealed

The U.S. Supreme Court

The Supreme Court is the highest court in the United States. The Court was created as part of the Constitutional Convention in 1787 and established in 1789 when Congress passed the Judiciary Act.

The Court is overseen by a chief justice and several associate justices. From 1789 to 1807, there were six justices. By 1863, four more had been added. Since 1869, the number of justices has been set at nine.

The Court receives approximately 10,000 requests for lower-court decision review during a term, which usually runs from October through June. Of these thousands of requests, the justices hear a limited number of cases pertaining to the Constitution and federal law. From October through April, the Court hears arguments two weeks of the month on Mondays, Tuesdays, and Wednesdays. During arguments, each side has 30 minutes to present its case. Much of the time may be taken answering justices' questions. The Court may take weeks or months before handing down a decision.

to her mother and brother that they should prepare to fly last-minute to Washington DC because she might be nominated.

The following Monday, May 25, the president's staff continued to work on the process involved in naming a nominee to the Supreme Court. This included conferring with medical personnel about Sotomayor's diabetes. The president had to feel certain that her diabetes would not interfere with her ability to carry out her duties as a justice. That evening, Obama shared his choice for nominee with the members of his staff. Next, he called that person and offered her the position.

On May 26, 2009, the president nominated Sotomayor to fill the seat vacated by Souter. During his nominating speech at the White House, Obama spoke of Sotomayor's credentials, including her attendance at two of the nation's top universities and years as a lawyer and a judge.

The Second Amendment

One critical issue that was debated after Sotomayor's nomination revolved around the Second Amendment to the U.S. Constitution. The amendment guarantees Americans the right to own guns: "A well regulated militia, being necessary to the security of a free state, the right of the people to keep and bear arms, shall not be infringed."[1]

Some conservatives stressed their feelings that Sotomayor would work to restrict that right. The National Rifle Association, which has been the most vocal pro-gun group, expressed that belief. Others who back the rights of gun owners found no reason to fear her. The American Hunters and Shooters Association came out in favor of Sotomayor.

When speaking about her most recent position on the U.S. Court of Appeals for the Second Circuit, Obama mentioned the effects of Sotomayor's work on her colleagues:

> For the past 11 years, she has been a judge on . . . one of the most demanding circuits in the country. There, she has handed down decisions on a range of constitutional and legal questions that are notable for their careful reasoning, earning the respect of colleagues on the bench, the admiration of many lawyers who argue cases in her court, and the adoration of her clerks, who look to her as a mentor.[2]

HER QUALIFICATIONS

During his speech, Obama stressed the importance of Sotomayor's experiences as a Latina and how important they were in shaping her as a person. Some took this to mean that these experiences would sway her decisions away from interpreting the law as it should be. This led both the president and his nominee into disfavor with those who considered her job would be to interpret the law—no more and no less. These people believed her experiences—or any nominee's experiences— should not factor into a justice's decision-making

*Sotomayor, right, meets with Senate Judiciary
Committee Chairman Senator Patrick Leahy.*

process. The president was trying to make the point,
however, that as human beings, we learn from
our experiences—whatever they may be, they must
naturally affect our reactions and decisions. He said,

> *For as Supreme Court Justice Oliver Wendell Holmes
> once said, the life of the law has not been logic, it has been
> experience; experience being tested by obstacles and barriers,
> by hardship and misfortune; experience insisting, persisting,
> and ultimately overcoming those barriers. It is experience that*

can give a person a common touch and a sense of compassion, an understanding of how the world works and how ordinary people live.

And that is why it is a necessary ingredient in the kind of justice we need on the Supreme Court.[3]

Sotomayor accepted the challenge offered by the president. During her nomination speech on May 26, Sotomayor spoke of her experiences:

This wealth of experiences, personal and professional, has helped me appreciate the variety of perspectives that present themselves in every case that I hear. It has helped me to understand, respect and respond to the concerns and arguments of all litigants who appear before me, as well as to the views of my colleagues on the bench.[4]

She also expressed the honor she felt in having been nominated. She thanked her family and colleagues. Then, she spoke about the daunting tasks and responsibilities that would be ahead of her if she was indeed confirmed:

I chose to be a lawyer, and ultimately a judge, because I find endless challenges in the complexities of the law. I firmly believe in the rule of law as the foundation of all of our basic rights.

For as long as I can remember, I have been inspired by the achievement of our founding fathers. They set forth principles that have endured for more than two centuries. Those principles are as meaningful and relevant in each generation as the generation before. It would be a profound privilege for me to play a role in applying those principles to the questions and controversies we face today.[5]

MAKING THE ROUNDS

Next, Sotomayor would have to take part in confirmation hearings, a process all Supreme Court justice nominees must endure. During the hearings, senators would ask her questions, challenge her, and allow Sotomayor to defend her record—all while the nation watches. Sotomayor had already spoken with some members of the Senate Judiciary Committee, which oversees the confirmation hearings. She called others, making the rounds to introduce herself to those who would determine her fate and the future of the U.S. Supreme Court.

Losing Hispanic-American Support

Critics claim that Bush could have helped the Republican Party regain Hispanic support by nominating Sotomayor to the Supreme Court. Two justices announced their retirement, but the president nominated two men: John G. Roberts was appointed chief justice in September 2005, and Samuel Alito Jr. became a justice in January 2006.

She was fortunate that Democrats controlled the Senate. The 2004 and 2008 elections had greatly swung the balance of power. Sotomayor had another reason to be confident in her appointment. The Republicans who were against her could not block her confirmation through a filibuster.

A filibuster—for example, making long, uninterrupted speeches to kill time—is a tactic that one party uses to delay Congress from acting on an issue. Finally, the Republicans on the committee had supported Sotomayor when she was appointed to the U.S. Court of Appeals for the Second Circuit in 1998.

None of this meant Sotomayor's confirmation would come easily. Sotomayor and her career as a judge would be scrutinized and criticized. Even the slightest mistake in defending herself or answering questions from members of the Senate Judiciary Committee could cost her a place on the Supreme Court. ⌐

Sotomayor's Speech

Before leaving New York City for Washington DC to attend her official nomination, Sotomayor e-mailed her acceptance speech to the White House. Obama's staff needed to review and approve her speech—and make changes, if necessary. Staff aides printed the final speech and placed it in a book at the podium where Sotomayor accepted Obama's nomination and gave her own speech. The staff members jumbled the pages, leaving them in the wrong order. But this did not cause a problem for Sotomayor—she had memorized her speech.

Members of the Senate Judiciary Committee, left to right:
Jeff Sessions, Edward Kaufman, and Patrick Leahy

*Sotomayor answered many questions during the Senate
Judiciary Committee's confirmation hearings.*

THE CONFIRMATION
HEARINGS

Sonia Sotomayor spent some of the first
day of her confirmation hearings trying
to dissipate fears that she would attempt to make
political changes as a Supreme Court justice. During
her opening statement to the Senate Judiciary

Committee on July 12, 2009, she emphasized that she would apply the law rather than make laws.

She did not dismiss her upbringing and early career as possible motivations in her decision-making processes. But she tied those experiences to enforcing the law:

> I saw children exploited and abused. I felt the suffering of victim's families torn apart by a loved one's needless death. And I learned the tough job law enforcement has protecting the public safety. . . . My personal and professional experiences help me listen and understand, with the law always commanding the result in every case.[1]

In doing so, she hoped to calm those who suspected that she would be an activist judge. Senator Jeff Sessions, the leading Republican on the committee, wasted no time expressing his belief that Sotomayor was not being completely truthful.

The Death Penalty

The death penalty was one of many issues raised during Sotomayor's confirmation hearings. The United States banned the death penalty for a short time in the early 1970s. While working for the Puerto Rican Legal Defense and Education Fund in 1981, Sotomayor signed a document opposing a bill that would restore the death penalty in New York. The document stated that the death penalty is associated with racism because it is applied more to minorities and the poor. New York restored the death penalty in 1995 and eliminated it again in 2007.

He said he was troubled by some of her past rulings and worried she would allow her sympathies to cloud her judgments.

Sessions could not change the feeling of most of his colleagues that Sotomayor was certain for confirmation. Republican Lindsey Graham even joked to Sotomayor that a spot on the Supreme Court was all but assured, but Sessions remained confrontational:

She has said her own background in feelings, sympathies, even prejudices are naturally going to have an impact

The Confirmation Process

The U.S. Constitution requires the Senate to confirm, or approve, Supreme Court justice nominees. The Senate is involved in other appointments as well, including high-level cabinet positions such as the secretaries of state, defense, and the treasury. More than 2,000 positions filled by presidential appointments require Senate involvement, but the cabinet secretaries and Supreme Court justices receive the greatest attention.

Almost all appointments are approved. The president submits a nomination in writing to the Senate. It is read on the floor of the Senate, but it is not voted on the same day. Sometimes, the nomination receives unanimous consent—all members vote in favor of the candidate. In this case, he or she is approved immediately. This has never been the case with Supreme Court justice nominees.

The nomination is referred to the committee, or group of senators, in charge of the position at hand. In the case of Supreme Court justices, this is the Senate Judiciary Committee. Confirmation hearings are held by the Senate to accept or reject a nominee for a high-ranking position. The hearings are open to the public. Those who support or oppose the nomination may be permitted to testify in front of the committee. After the hearings, the nomination goes to the entire U.S. Senate for a vote.

on how she rules in cases. That's directly contrary to the American ideal that every judge must put aside their personal feelings, backgrounds, prejudices and render justice to each party in that case. [2]

THE BATTLE RESUMES

The second day of hearings brought more criticism, this time from Graham, who questioned Sotomayor's disposition as a judge. Graham listed some anonymous complaints compiled in a book of judicial profiles:

She's a terror on the bench. She's temperamental, excitable, she seems angry. She's overall aggressive, not very judicial. She does not have a very good temperament. She abuses lawyers. . . . [S]he behaves in an out-of-control manner. She makes inappropriate outbursts. She's nasty to lawyers. She will attack lawyers for making an argument she does not like. She can be a bit of a bully. [3]

But no lawyer ever registered or put a complaint on record against Sotomayor, who responded that she does ask lawyers tough questions when they are presenting cases to her. She added that she also gives them time to explain their positions and to sway her to their side. She denied a problem with her temper,

Defending the Defense Fund

During the confirmation process, Sonia Sotomayor defended her work with the Puerto Rican Legal Defense and Education Fund. Founded in 1972 to fight for the civil rights of Puerto Rican Americans, Sotomayor joined the organization in 1980. She was particularly active during her 12 years as a volunteer. Some senators suggested that her kinship and support for Puerto Rican Americans would influence her decisions as a Supreme Court justice. But Sotomayor is not the first minority justice to fight for racial equality and justice. African American Thurgood Marshall worked as a lawyer for the National Association for the Advancement of Colored People Legal Defense and Education Fund in the 1950s and 1960s.

stating that she boasts positive relationships with attorneys and her fellow judges.

Graham's assertions motivated the Democrats on the Senate Judiciary Committee, all of whom supported Sotomayor, to fight back. They claimed that criticism of her had no basis in fact. Graham continued his attack, moving on to Sotomayor's most controversial statement of all. In a 2001 speech, she had contended that a wise Latina woman who has experienced what she had could judge cases better than a white male who had not.

The Republican senator claimed that a white male would lose his job if he made a similar statement. Sotomayor claimed her remarks were misunderstood and should be considered based on her background. She appeased her critics, including those who claimed that she would allow her personal opinions to cloud her judgment:

Sotomayor was sworn in before testifying at her nomination hearing.

[W]ithout doubt, I do not believe that any ethnic, racial or gender group has an advantage in sound judging. I do believe that every person has an equal opportunity to be a good and wise judge, regardless of their background or life experiences. [The statement was] bad because it left an impression that I believe that life experiences commanded a result. . . . The process of judging is the process of keeping an open mind. At no time have I permitted my personal views to influence a case.[4]

> "There are some people in Congress who would criticize severely anyone President Obama nominated. They'll seize on any handle. One is that she's a woman, another is that she made the remark about Latina women. And I thought it was ridiculous for them to make a big deal out of that. Think of how many times you've said something that you didn't get out quite right, and you would edit your statement if you could. I'm sure she meant no more than what I mean when I say: Yes, women bring a different life experience to the table. All of our differences make the conference better."[5]
>
> —*Supreme Court Justice Ruth Bader Ginsburg*

ANOTHER DAY, MORE QUESTIONS

As the hearings continued to the third day, Sotomayor became more guarded in her answers to the committee. She declined to answer questions about her personal opinions regarding such controversial topics as abortion and the constitutional rights to own guns.

Republican Senator Tom Coburn brought up a 1992 case that Sotomayor had reaffirmed a woman's right to have an abortion as decided by *Roe v. Wade* 19 years earlier. Coburn, a physician and antiabortion advocate who said that he had delivered more than 4,000 babies, asked Sotomayor her feelings about abortions in various medical situations. When she responded to Coburn, Sotomayor stated that she would make decisions based on past rulings. "We don't make policy choices in the court," she insisted. "We look at the case before us with the interests that are argued by the parties, look at our precedent, and try to apply its principles to the arguments parties are raising."[6]

Coburn had no more luck trying to extract Sotomayor's views on the Second Amendment, which guarantees Americans the right to bear arms. She spoke about a 2008 Supreme Court decision that overturned a law restricting handgun ownership in Washington DC in affirming those rights. She reiterated that judges do not make laws; they simply base their decisions on the Constitution and precedents set in past rulings. Sotomayor also stated that interpretation of the law can change as society changes and new knowledge is gained on certain issues.

Sotomayor continued to answer questions about her most controversial statements and decisions to the satisfaction of the Senate Judiciary Committee.

Broken Ankle

Not only was Sotomayor challenged emotionally and mentally by the strain of being a Supreme Court nominee, but she had to overcome a minor physical problem as well. She had a broken ankle. Sotomayor had tripped at LaGuardia Airport in New York in early June. The fall caused a small fracture, and Sotomayor had to use crutches until her ankle healed.

On July 28, 2009, the committee voted to send
her confirmation to the full Senate for final
consideration. Graham said,

> *I gladly give her my vote because I think she meets the
> qualifications test. . . . And if she, by being a woman on the
> court, will inspire young women, particularly Latino women
> to seek a career in the law, that would be a good thing.*[7]

Sotomayor certainly agreed.

U.S. Supreme Court building

Sotomayor's mother held the Bible on which her daughter was sworn in as a Supreme Court justice.

CONFIRMED!

After her confirmation hearing, Sonia Sotomayor had only one thing left to do: wait. She had done all she could in support of her nomination to the Supreme Court. Now, it was time for the Senate to vote. On August 6, 2009,

Sotomayor was confirmed by the United States Senate in a 68–31 vote. The vote was not strictly along party lines. Nine Republicans voted in favor of Sotomayor.

But the final outcome was never in doubt. And when the last vote had been counted, President Obama spoke glowingly about the woman he had nominated:

> With this historic vote, the Senate has affirmed that Judge Sotomayor has the intellect, the temperament, the history, the integrity and the independence of mind to ably serve on our nation's highest court. . . . These core American ideals—justice, equality, and opportunity—are the very ideals that have made Judge Sotomayor's own uniquely American journey possible. They're ideals she's fought for throughout her career, and the ideals the Senate has upheld today in breaking yet another barrier and moving us yet another step closer to a more perfect union.[1]

Not Always Confirmed

Not all Supreme Court nominees have been confirmed. In 1811, President James Madison nominated Alexander Wolcott. The Senate turned him down by the most lopsided vote in U.S. history: 24–9.

Perhaps the most famous rejection was Robert Bork. Nominated by President Ronald Reagan in 1987, he was deemed too conservative. The Senate Judiciary Committee rejected him after 12 days of hearings. Reagan's next nominee, Douglas Ginsburg, was withdrawn because he had admitted to smoking marijuana.

Harriet Miers was another failed candidate. Nominated by President George W. Bush in 2005, she withdrew her name due to widespread criticism that she was not qualified.

The Abortion Debate

The abortion debate began in earnest in 1973 when the U.S. Supreme Court's decision in *Roe v. Wade* legalized abortion. The Court ruled that abortions could be performed on fetuses that could not live outside the womb.

Those against abortion are called "pro-life" believers. They claim that a fetus is a human being from the time it is conceived and that, therefore, abortion is murder. On the opposite side of the issue are "pro-choice" advocates. They believe it is the right of every woman to decide whether abortion is the proper choice for her—it is not the government's decision. Future Supreme Court decisions may decide whether abortions remain legal, which is why Sotomayor's opinion on the matter is important to so many.

That sentiment was certainly felt by many of the nation's 45 million Hispanic Americans. Hispanic women celebrated Sotomayor's confirmation, particularly supporters from the Puerto Rican Legal Defense and Education Fund. Some who watched the Senate vote from the organization's New York headquarters wore T-shirts printed with "Wise Latina," the phrase Sotomayor used in 2001 that elicited such criticism.

Sworn In

The 55-year-old Sotomayor was sworn in twice on August 8, 2009. In a private ceremony, she placed her hand on a Bible and pledged to support and defend the Constitution. Moments later, she was escorted to the office of Chief Justice John Roberts where she pledged to impart equal justice to both the rich and the poor.

The brief ceremonies made her appointment official. What Sotomayor had achieved was beyond even her wildest dreams as a child engrossed by Nancy Drew and then Perry Mason. On September 9, she donned her new black robe at a special Supreme Court induction with President Obama. Sotomayor was sworn in yet again by Chief Justice Roberts, though it was merely a ritual this time. She then took a seat at the far left of the bench, the spot reserved for the newest justice. The ceremonies

The U.S. Constitution

The U.S. Constitution is the result of the Articles of the Confederation, which was created in 1781. The document came from heated debate between 55 delegates in Philadelphia, Pennsylvania, during the Constitutional Convention. The delegates' biggest concerns were power and freedom. They wanted to avoid a monarchy similar to that of England. They also wanted to ensure citizens' freedom. Other issues included slavery, representation, and states' rights. Delegates from northern states and southern states had different ideas about slavery. And those from states of different sizes disagreed about how many representatives each state should have.

The solution to the debate was to have a Senate, in which each state would have an equal number of representatives, and a House of Representatives, in which representation would be based on state populations. Following further changes, the Constitution was submitted for ratification on September 28, 1787. Nine of America's 13 states had to approve the Constitution for it to be formally accepted. Ratification was the result of a promise that a bill of rights would be added to the Constitution. In September 1789, Congress proposed 12 amendments. Ten were ratified and became the Bill of Rights. They were formally adopted on December 15, 1791.

ended as she joined Roberts on a stroll down the front steps of the Supreme Court, where photographers snapped one picture after another.

The months of waiting since her nomination and the formalities were finally over. Associate Justice Sotomayor wasted no time attending to the business of her new role. She began working on her first Supreme Court case that day.

HER FIRST TERM

The Supreme Court began its new term on October 5. Sotomayor proved an active questioner during her first few months as an associate justice. As of December 2009, she had asked 146 questions compared to 110 for Chief Justice Roberts.

The Court released its first four decisions of the 2009–2010 term in early December. The first of these was delivered by the newest justice

"Wise Latina"

The "Wise Latina" phrase Sotomayor uttered during a 2001 speech that prompted so much criticism was soon emblazoned on more than a few T-shirts. By the summer of 2009, the phrase was also seen on coffee mugs, baby bibs, and even coats made for dogs. Though Sotomayor distanced herself from the remark during the hearings, other Hispanics ran with it. Texas senator Leticia Van de Putte had 200 T-shirts reading "Another wise Latina woman" made and sent to friends, relatives, and fellow politicians. Sotomayor, however, has expressed regret that people are making money off her statement.

As a Supreme Court justice, Sotomayor rules on only cases regarding federal legislation and the Constitution.

on December 8. It was Sotomayor's first opinion in her new role. The ruling was on the case *Mohawk v. Carpenter*. The case focused on the issue of attorney-client privilege, and the justices unanimously agreed with the lower court's ruling in favor of Carpenter.

In 2009, Sotomayor, back right, became the first Hispanic woman to serve as a justice on the U.S. Supreme Court.

None of the first four cases could be considered monumental, though Sotomayor did make a small imprint with her written opinion on one case when she used the term "undocumented immigrant" rather than the more common *illegal immigrant* to describe a person who was living in the United States without the required documentation.[2]

A few weeks later, Sotomayor delivered a ruling that was more noteworthy. On January 21, 2010, she wrote her first full opinion as a justice on the case *Wood v. Alley*. The case did not set legal precedent, but it was notable because of Sotomayor's decision. While Sotomayor has a long judicial record, there is little in it regarding capital punishment.

In the 7–2 ruling, Sotomayor and six other justices upheld the death penalty for Holly Wood, an inmate in Alabama found guilty of shooting and killing his ex-girlfriend. Wood was appealing his sentence. He noted his lawyer's decision to not present evidence in a psychologist's report about Wood's mental limitations as evidence during his trial.

Sotomayor wrote in the Court's ruling,

> *Even if it is debatable, it is not unreasonable to conclude that . . . counsel made a strategic decision not to inquire further into the information contained in the report about Wood's mental deficiencies and not to present to the jury such information.*[4]

No Romantic Life

Sotomayor admitted in late 2009 to reporters in Puerto Rico that her new job as Supreme Court justice has pretty much squelched her romantic life. "I understand from my girlfriends that I've been put on a most-eligible bachelorette list," she said. "But right now I pity the man who tries to find a minute in my schedule."[3]

In addition, Sotomayor noted that the psychologist's report noted that Wood tried to kill another ex-girlfriend.

It remains to be seen if Sotomayor will be involved in a decision that affects the direction of heatedly debated issues such as abortion, affirmative action, and Second Amendment rights. What is certain is that a first-generation Puerto Rican-American girl from the New York City housing projects has become a Supreme Court justice and that her achievement affirms that the United States is indeed a land of opportunity. ⌣

Sonia Sotomayor, Supreme Court justice

TIMELINE

1954	1957	1963
Sonia Sotomayor is born on June 25 in New York City.	Sotomayor and her parents move to Bronxdale Houses, a housing project in the Bronx area of New York City.	Sotomayor is diagnosed with diabetes; her father dies.

1980	1980	1982
Sotomayor begins working as an attorney at the Manhattan district attorney's office in August.	Sotomayor earns a spot on the board of directors of the Puerto Rican Legal Defense and Education Fund.	Sotomayor works as a prosecutor and survives danger by gathering evidence for the Tarzan Burglar case.

1972

Sotomayor graduates as valedictorian from Cardinal Spellman High School in June.

1976

Sotomayor graduates with top honors from Princeton University in June with a degree in history.

1979

Sotomayor graduates from Yale Law School in June.

1984

The Manhattan law firm Pavia & Harcourt hires Sotomayor, who enters the private practice on April 26.

1991

President George H. W. Bush nominates Sotomayor to the U.S. District Court for the Southern District of New York.

1992

Sotomayor is confirmed as a judge on the U.S. District Court for the Southern District of New York in June.

TIMELINE

1993

Sotomayor rules that a suicide note left by White House Counsel Vincent Foster had to be released to the *Wall Street Journal*.

1995

Sotomayor helps end the Major League Baseball players' strike by granting an injunction against the team owners on March 30.

1997

President Bill Clinton nominates Sotomayor to the U.S. Court of Appeals for the Second Circuit on June 25.

2009

President Barack Obama nominates Sotomayor to the U.S. Supreme Court on May 26.

2009

The Senate Judiciary Committee begins confirmation hearings on the Sotomayor nomination on July 13.

2009

Sotomayor is confirmed on August 6.

1998

The Senate confirms Sotomayor as a judge to the U.S. Court of Appeals for the Second Circuit on October 2.

2001

On October 26, Sotomayor makes a statement about being a wise Latina woman that sparks controversy.

2008

Sotomayor rules in favor of New Haven Mayor John DeStefano in *Ricci v. DeStefano*, a case dealing with racial discrimination.

2009

Sotomayor is sworn in twice as a Supreme Court justice, in private and public ceremonies, on August 8.

2009

Sotomayor officially dons her judicial robe for the first time on September 9 to be photographed on the Supreme Court's front steps.

2009

Sotomayor begins serving her first term on the Supreme Court on October 5.

ESSENTIAL FACTS

DATE OF BIRTH

June 25, 1954

PLACE OF BIRTH

New York, New York

PARENTS

Juan and Celina Sotomayor

EDUCATION

Cardinal Spellman High School, Princeton University, Yale Law School

MARRIAGE

Kevin Edward Noonan (1976–1983)

CHILDREN

None

CAREER HIGHLIGHTS

Sotomayor began working for the Manhattan district attorney in August 1979, two months after she received her law degree. In this position, she did extensive work with people on the streets, including investigating cases with police officers. After five years working on public cases in this role, Sotomayor took a position with Pavia & Harcourt, a private law firm. In 1992, Sotomayor's

dream of becoming a judge was realized when she was appointed
to the U.S. District Court for the Southern District of New York.
In this position, she made noteworthy rulings in separate cases
regarding a suicide note and Major League Baseball. In 1998,
Sotomayor became a judge on the U.S. Court of Appeals for the
Second Circuit. In 2009, she became the first female Hispanic
Supreme Court justice.

SOCIETAL CONTRIBUTION

As a lawyer for the district attorney's office in Manhattan,
Sotomayor fought crime. As a judge, she has worked to uphold and
interpret the ideals of the U.S. Constitution and legislation to rule
fairly and impartially.

CONFLICTS

Republican senators questioned Sotomayor's suitability as a
Supreme Court justice, though their challenges did not prevent her
appointment to the position in 2009.

QUOTE

"I chose to be a lawyer, and ultimately a judge, because I find
endless challenges in the complexities of the law. I firmly believe in
the rule of law as the foundation of all of our basic rights.

For as long as I can remember, I have been inspired by the
achievement of our founding fathers. They set forth principles
that have endured for more than two centuries. Those principles
are as meaningful and relevant in each generation as the generation
before. It would be a profound privilege for me to play a role in
applying those principles to the questions and controversies we
face today." —*Sonia Sotomayor, in her Supreme Court nomination speech,
May 26, 2009*

ADDITIONAL RESOURCES

SELECT BIBLIOGRAPHY

Barnes, Robert, and Michael A. Fletcher. "Riskiest Choice on Obama's List Embodies His Criteria." *Washington Post Online*. 27 May 2009 <http://www.washingtonpost.com/wp-dyn/content/article/2009/05/26/AR2009052600889.html?sid=ST2009052600912>.

Hoffman, Jan. "A Breakthrough Judge: What She Always Wanted." *New York Times Online*. 25 Sept. 1992 <http://www.nytimes.com/1992/09/25/news/a-breakthrough-judge-what-she-always-wanted.html?pagewanted=1>.

Sotomayor, Sonia. "Opening statement before the Senate Judiciary Committee." *United States Senate Committee on the Judiciary Online*. 13 July 2009 <http://judiciary.senate.gov/hearings/testimony.cfm?id=3959&wit_id=8102>.

Winn, Peter. "The Education of Sonia Sotomayor." *Washington Post Online*. 12 July 2009 <http://www.washingtonpost.com/wp-dyn/content/article/2009/07/09/AR2009070902391.html>.

FURTHER READING

Brannen, Daniel, and Richard Clay Hanes. *Supreme Court Drama: Cases That Changed America*. Farmington Hills, MI: UXL, 2000.

Giddens-White, Bryon. *The Supreme Court and the Judicial Branch*. Chicago, IL: Heinemann Library, 2006.

Isaacs, Sally Senzell. *Understanding the U.S. Constitution*. New York, NY: Crabtree, 2009.

Web Links

To learn more about Sonia Sotomayor, visit ABDO Publishing Company online at **www.abdopublishing.com**. Web sites about Sonia Sotomayor are featured on our Book Links page. These links are routinely monitored and updated to provide the most current information available.

Places To Visit

Hispanic Society of America

613 W. 155th Street, New York, NY 10032
212-926-2234
www.hispanicsociety.org/hispanic/visitor.htm
Learn about Hispanic culture in the United States and elsewhere at this free museum, which features artwork, photographs, and other collections.

LatinoJustice PRLDEF

99 Hudson Street 14th Floor, New York, NY 10013-2815
212-219-3360, 800-328-2322
http://latinojustice.org/
Formerly the Puerto Rican Legal Defense and Education Fund, this is where Sonia Sotomayor worked as a volunteer for several years. LatinoJustice PRLDEF continues to work for and with Latinos to help them achieve personally and professionally as individuals, families, and communities.

Supreme Court Building

First and E Capitol Streets NE, Washington, DC 20002
202-479-3000
http://tourofdc.org/tours/SupremeCourt/
Visitors can listen to Supreme Court oral arguments on the first two Mondays, Tuesdays, and Wednesdays of each month. Short tours last three to five minutes, or visitors can witness the entire proceedings.

GLOSSARY

activist
> When referring to a judge, one who makes rulings based on beliefs in particular causes or political issues.

appeal
> Legal action taken after a court decision has been made to have the case heard by a higher court in the hope that the original decision will be reversed.

appointment
> A position that is not achieved through election but by being designated.

bar association
> A professional organization for lawyers made up of a particular bar, such as a state.

confirmation
> The accepting of a presidential judicial nominee by the U.S. Senate.

conservative
> An individual who supports particular political policies, most often advocating stringent economic policies and taking stands against abortion, gun control, and affirmative action.

courts of appeals
> In the hierarchy of the U.S. federal judicial system, the courts between the district courts, where trials take place, and the Supreme Court.

hearing
> An examination and discussion of the evidence in a particular case.

Hispanic
> An individual of Spanish or Latin American descent.

injunction
> A judicial order directed to require an individual to do or stop doing a particular act.

justice
> A judge who sits on the Supreme Court.

Latina
> A Hispanic female.

minority
> A person whose ethnicity, race, or religious belief is not among the majority in a particular geographic area.

nominate
> To propose an individual for a position that will be decided upon by a debate and vote of others.

objectivity
> The ability to keep personal beliefs from entering into making decisions or rulings.

precedent
> In law, a previous case decision used to help decide the outcome of a current case.

prosecutor
> The attorney who represents the government in court and often attempts to establish the guilt of an individual on trial.

ruling
> The final decision made by a judge.

strike
> The action taken by workers who stop working in an attempt to force employers to negotiate better pay, working conditions, or other upgrades to their employment.

U.S. Supreme Court
> The highest court in the United States.

Source Notes

Chapter 1. Controversial Call

1. Charlie Savage. "A Judge's View of Judging Is on the Record." *NYTimes.com*. 15 May 2009. 20 Feb. 2010 <http://www.nytimes.com/2009/05/15/us/15judge.html>.

2. Ibid.

3. "Honorable Mario G. Olmos Law & Cultural Diversity Memorial Lecture." *UC Berkeley School of Law online*. 28 Apr. 2010 <http://www.law.berkeley.edu/2569.htm>.

4. Nina Totenberg. "Is Sonia Sotomayor Mean?" *NPR.org*. 15 June 2009. 5 Apr. 2010 <http://www.npr.org/templates/story/story.php?storyId=105343155>.

5. Bill Mears. "Sotomayor says she was 'perfect affirmative action baby.'" *CNN.com*. 11 June 2009. 6 Apr. 2010 <http://www.cnn.com/2009/POLITICS/06/11/sotomayor.affirmative.action/index.html>.

6. FindLaw. "*RICCI* et al. v. *De*STEFANO et al." 2010. 11 Apr. 2010 <http://caselaw.lp.findlaw.com/scripts/getcase.pl?court=US&vol=000&invol=07-1428>.

7. Robert Barnes and Michael A. Fletcher. "Riskiest Choice on Obama's List Embodies His Criteria." *WashingtonPost.com*. 27 May 2009. 6 Apr. 2010 <http://www.washingtonpost.com/wp-dyn/content/article/2009/05/26/AR2009052600889.html?sid=ST2009052600912>.

8. Sonia Sotomayor. "Opening statement before the Senate Judiciary Committee." *Senate.gov*. 13 July 2009. 5 Apr. 2010 <http://judiciary.senate.gov/hearings/testimony.cfm?id=3959&wit_id=8102>.

Chapter 2. Young Sonia

1. Sonia Sotomayor. "A Latin Judges Voice." *NYTimes.com*. 14 May 2009. 28 Apr. 2010. <http://www.nytimes.com/2009/05/15/us/politics/15judge.text.html>.

2. Ibid.

3. Robin Shulman. "Supreme Change." *WashingtonPost.com*. 16 June 2009. 20 Feb. 2010 <http://www.washingtonpost.com/wp-dyn/content/article/2009/06/15/AR2009061503170.html>.

4. Jan Hoffman. "A Breakthrough Judge: What She Always Wanted." *NYTimes.com*. 25 Sept. 1992. 7 Mar. 2010 <http://www.nytimes.com/1992/09/25/news/a-breakthrough-judge-what-she-always-wanted.html?pagewanted=all>.

5. "Sotomayor Confirmation Hearings, Day 3." *NYTimes.com.*
16 July 2009. 5 Apr. 2010 <http://www.nytimes.com/2009/07/15/us/
politics/15confirm-text.html?pagewanted=25>.
6. Jan Hoffman. "A Breakthrough Judge: What She Always Wanted."
NYTimes.com. 25 Sept. 1992. 7 Mar. 2010 <http://www.nytimes.com/
1992/09/25/news/a-breakthrough-judge-what-she-always-wanted.
html?pagewanted=all>.

Chapter 3. Princeton and Yale
1. Peter Winn. "The Education of Sonia Sotomayor." *WashingtonPost.com.*
12 July 2009. 5 Apr. 2010 <http://www.washingtonpost.com/
wp-dyn/content/article/2009/07/09/AR2009070902391.html>.
2. Ruth Stevens. "Princeton gives highest awards to top students.
Princeton University Online. 24 Feb. 2007. 20 Feb. 2010
<http://www.princeton.edu/main/news/archive/S17/23/47M75/>.
3. Staff. "Germany, Sotomayor receive 1976 Pyne Prize (Feb. 28, 1976)."
Daily Princetonian Online. 29 May 2009. 20 Feb. 2010
<http://www.dailyprincetonian.com/2009/05/15/23735/>.
4. Elizabeth Landau. "Sotomayor 'always willing to speak up' at Yale Law."
CNN.com. 26 May 2009. 20 Feb. 2010 <http://www.cnn.com/2009/
POLITICS/05/26/sotomayor.princeton.yale/>.
5. Ibid.
6. Ibid.
7. Neil A. Lewis. "On a Supreme Court Prospect's Résumé: 'Baseball
Savior.'" *NYTimes.com.* 14 May 2009. 5 Apr. 2010
<http://www.nytimes.com/2009/05/15/us/15sotomayor.html?_r=1>.

Chapter 4. Launching Her Career
1. Ann O'Neill. "Sotomayor learned the ropes on 'Tarzan' case." *CNN.
com.* 28 July 2009. 20 Feb. 2010 <http://www.cnn.com/2009/US/07/16/
sotomayor.district.attorney/index.html>.
2. Ibid.
3. Ibid.
4. Karen Sloan. "Nominee's civil practice was with a small, but
specialized, firm." *Law.com.* 27 May 2009. 11 Apr. 2010
<http://www.law.com/jsp/nlj/PubArticleNLJ.
jsp?id=1202431011230&Nominees_civil_practice_was_with_a_small_
specialized_firm&sireturn=1>.

SOURCE NOTES CONTINUED

5. Serge F. Kovaleski. "Little Information Given About Solo Law Practice Run by Sotomayor in '80s." *NYTimes.com*. 6 July 2009. 4 May 2010. <http://www.nytimes.com/2009/07/07/us/politics/07firm.html>.

Chapter 5. Achieving Her Dream
1. Jan Hoffman. "A Breakthrough Judge: What She Always Wanted. *NYTimes.com*. 25 Sept. 1992. 11 April 2010 <http://www.nytimes.com/1992/09/25/news/a-breakthrough-judge-what-she-always-wanted.html?pagewanted=1>.
2. Richard Sandomir. "Sotomayor's Baseball Ruling Lingers, 14 Years Later." *NYTimes.com*. 26 May 2009. 6 Apr. 2010 <http://www.nytimes.com/2009/05/27/sports/baseball/27sandomir.html>.

Chapter 6. A New Nomination
1. Neil A. Lewis. "G.O.P., It's Eyes on High Court, Blocks a Judge." *NYTimes.com*. 13 June 1998. 20 Feb. 2010 <http://www.nytimes.com/1998/06/13/nyregion/gop-its-eyes-on-high-court-blocks-a-judge.html>.
2. Sonia Sotomayor. "A Latin Judges Voice." *NYTimes.com*. 14 May 2009. 28 Apr. 2010. <http://www.nytimes.com/2009/05/15/us/politics/15judge.text.html>.
3. Thomas Sowell. "The Statue of Justice Wears a Blindfold." *RealClearPolitics.com*. 7 May 2009. 20 Feb. 2010 <http://www.realclearpolitics.com/articles/2009/05/07/empathy_versus_law_part_iii_96334.html>.
4. Yvonne Nava and Leanne Gendreau. "Sotomayor Ruled in 'D-Bag Case.'" *NBCConnecticut.com*. 1 June 2009. 6 Apr. 2010 <http://www.nbcconnecticut.com/news/local-beat/Critics-unhappy-with-Sotomayors-role-in-CT-free-speech-case.html>.

Chapter 7. Supreme Court Justice Nomination
1. "Bill of Rights." *Cornell University Law School Online*. 6 Apr. 2010 <http://topics.law.cornell.edu/constitution/billofrights>.
2. "Transcript of Obama-Sotomayor Announcement." *CNN.com*. 26 May 2009. 20 Feb. 2010 <http://www.cnn.com/2009/POLITICS/05/26/obama.sotomayor.transcript/index.html>.
3. Ibid.
4. "Full Text: Judge Sonia Sotomayor's Speech." *Time.com*. 26 May 2009. 21 Feb. 2010 <http://www.time.com/time/politics/article/0,8599,1900940,00.html>.

5. Ibid.

Chapter 8. The Confirmation Hearings
1. Ariane de Vogue and Jan Crawford Greenburg. "Sotomayor Pledges 'Fidelity to the Law'." *ABCNews.com*. 13 July 2009. 20 Feb. 2010 <http://abcnews.go.com/print?id=8065546>.
2. Ibid.
3. Ariane de Vogue and Theresa Cook. "Supreme Court Nominee a 'Bully on the Bench?'" *ABCNews.com*. 14 July 2009. 20 Feb. 2010 <http://abcnews.go.com/print?id=8074756>.
4. Ibid.
5. Emily Bazelon. "The Place of Women on the Court." *NYTimes.com*. July 2009. 20 Feb. 2010 <http://www.nytimes.com/2009/07/12/magazine/12ginsburg-t.html?pagewanted=1&_r=1>.
6. "Sen. Coburn Questions Judge Sotomayor at Supreme Court Nomination Hearings." *WashingtonPost.com*. 15 July 2009. 6 Apr. 2010 <http://www.washingtonpost.com/wp-dyn/content/article/2009/07/15/AR2009071501414.html>.
7. Theresa Cook. "Sonia Sotomayor One Step closer to confirmation vote." *ABCNews.com*. 28 July 2009. 24 June 2010 <http://abcnews.go.com/print?id=81911367>.

Chapter 9. Confirmed!
1. Katherine Brandon. "Justice Sonia Sotomayor." *The White House Blog*. 6 Aug. 2009. 6 Apr. 2010 <http://www.whitehouse.gov/blog/Justice-Sonia-Sotomayor>.
2. Adam Liptak. "Sotomayor Draws Retort From a Fellow Justice." *NYTimes.com*. 9 Dec. 2009. 20 Feb. 2010 <http://www.nytimes.com/2009/12/09/us/09sotomayor.html>.
3. David Saltonstall. "Justice Sonia Sotomayor looking for law not love; still humbled by appointment." *NYDailyNews*.com. 19 Dec. 2009. 20 Feb. 2010 <http://www.nydailynews.com/news/2009/12/19/2009-12-19_for_sonia_men_v_court_is_no_contest.html>.
4. Robert Barnes. "In a first test for court watchers, Sotomayor upholds death sentence." *WashingtonPost.com*. 21 Jan. 2010. 10 May 2010 <http://www.washingtonpost.com/wp-dyn/content/article/2010/01/20/AR2010012004599.html>.

INDEX

abortion, 56, 58, 59–60, 82, 88, 94
affirmative action, 11–12, 94

bar exam, 36, 39, 41
baseball strike, 50–52
Bill of Rights, 48, 89
Bronxdale Houses, 19, 20, 23
Bush, George H. W., 47–48
Bush, George W., 59–60, 64, 65, 73, 87

Cardi, Dawn, 38
Cardinal Spellman High School, 24
Carter, Stephen, 31–32
Center for Reproductive Law and Policy v. Bush, 59–60
Clinton, Bill, 51, 55, 61
Coburn, Tom, 82–83
confirmation hearings, 62, 73, 76–85

death penalty, 77, 93
DeStefano, John, 8
diabetes, 21, 69
Doninger v. Niehoff, 60–62

Fehr, Donald, 51
Foster, Vincent, 48

Ginsburg, Douglas, 87
Ginsburg, Ruth Bader, 66, 82
Graham, Lindsey, 78, 79, 80, 84

Hispanic vote in 2008, 65–66
Holton v. Fraitellone, 56

Kagan, Elena, 67, 68
Kennedy, Anthony, 12
Klonoff, Robert, 31

Latino Students Organization, 30
Leahy, Patrick, 57

M. Taylor Pyne Honor Prize, 29, 30
Maddicks, Richard, 40–41
Mason, Perry, 23, 89
McCain, John, 65
Miers, Harriet, 87
Mohawk v. Carpenter, 91
Moynihan, Patrick, 47
Murray, Warren, 38

Nancy Drew books, 22, 89
Napolitano, Janet, 67, 68
1995 World Series, 50
Noonan, Kevin Edward (husband), 30, 42

Obama, Barack, 13, 65, 66–72, 74, 82, 87, 89
Orange, Taur, 20

Pappas v. Giuliani, 57–59, 60
Pavia & Harcourt, 42–44, 46–47
Perry Mason, 23, 47
Princeton University, 12, 26–30, 31, 34

Ricci, Frank, 8–9
Ricci v. DeStefano, 8–11
Roberts, John, 73, 88, 89, 90

Second Amendment, 69, 83, 94
Senate Judiciary Committee, 14, 48, 49, 57, 73, 74, 76–77, 78, 80, 83, 87
Shaw, Pittman, Potts & Trowbridge, 33
Skulnik, Steven, 43
Sotomayor, Celina (mother), 16–17, 20–22, 24, 69
Sotomayor, Juan (brother), 17, 19, 21, 22, 24, 69
Sotomayor, Juan (father), 16–17, 19–20
Sotomayor, Sonia
  birth, 12, 17
  career, 36–44, 46–52, 54–62, 64–74, 76–85, 86–94
  education, 21–22, 24, 26–34
  health, 19, 20, 23, 69, 83
Souter, David, 66, 69
Sowell, Thomas, 60

Tarzan Burglar, 39–42
Third World Center, 28, 30,
Trial Bureau 50, 37
Turley, Jonathan, 61–62

U.S. Constitution, 49, 69, 78, 89
U.S. Court of Appeals for the Second Circuit, 51, 54–62, 64, 70, 74
U.S. District Court for the Southern District of New York, 47–52, 49
University of California, Berkeley, 6, 7, 17, 59

Vento v. Lord, 56

Wall Street Journal, 48
wise Latina, 7, 80, 88, 90
Wolcott, Alexander, 87
Wood, Diane, 67, 68
Wood v. Alley, 93

Yale Law Journal, 31, 32
Yale Law School, 30, 33

Essential Lives

ABOUT THE AUTHOR

Martin Gitlin is a freelance writer who has written more than 20 educational books, including biographies about newspaper publisher Joseph Pulitzer and filmmaker Walt Disney and historical books about the Battle of the Little Bighorn, the stock market crash, and the landmark *Brown v. Board of Education* Supreme Court decision. Gitlin has won more than 45 awards during his 25 years as a writer, including first place for general excellence from the Associated Press. He lives with his wife and three children in Cleveland, Ohio.

PHOTO CREDITS

Collection of the Supreme Court of the United States, Steve Petteway/AP Images, cover, 3, 95; Pablo Martinez Monsivais/AP Images, 6, 81; Charles Dharapak/AP Images, 10, 76, 92; Alex Brandon/AP Images, 15; White House/AP Images, 16, 25, 26, 43, 96 (top); Bebeto Matthews/AP Images, 18, 22; Daniel Hulshizer /AP Images, 29; David Gunn/iStockphoto, 33; Bob Child/AP Images, 35; Mark Lennihan/AP Images, 36, 96; iStockphoto, 40, 46, 64; Robert Billstone/iStockphoto, 45, 97; Clark Jones / AP Images, 53; Jeffrey M. Boan/AP Images, 54, 98 (top); Nikolay Mamluke/iStockphoto, 58; Mark Lennihan /AP Images, 63; Susan Walsh /AP Images, 67, 98 (bottom); Harry Hamburg/AP Images, 71; Gerald Herbert/AP Images, 75; Michael DiBari Jr./AP Images, 85; J. Scott Applewhite/AP Images, 86, 99; Stefan Klein/ iStockphoto, 91